REE900. Gilbert, Adrian
1039   The Russian Revolution

05804

PIER Collection
Program in International Education Resources
Yale University
306 Henry Luce Hall
34 Hillhouse Avenue
New Haven. CT 06520

REVOLUTION!

THE RUSSIAN REVOLUTION

Adrian Gilbert

Thomson Learning
New York

REVOLUTION!

1848 Year of Revolution
The American Revolution
The Easter Rising
The French Revolution
Revolution in Europe 1989
The Russian Revolution

Cover: A dramatic painting of Lenin addressing the workers
Title page: A typically heroic communist depiction of Vladimir Ilyich Lenin, the leader of the Bolshevik Revolution
Opposite: The end of the old order—Russian children survey the broken statue of Czar Alexander III, father of the last Romanov czar, Nicholas II.

First published in the United States in 1996 by
Thomson Learning
New York, NY

Published simultaneously in Great Britain by Wayland (Publishers) Ltd.

U.S. copyright © 1996 Thomson Learning

U.K. copyright © 1995 Wayland Publishers Ltd.

Library of Congress Cataloging-in-Publication Data
Gilbert, Adrian.
The Russian revolution / Adrian Gilbert.
        p.   cm.—(Revolution!)
   Includes bibliographical references and index.
   Summary: Examines the causes, events, and aftermath of the 1917 revolution in Russia that led to the rise of Communism.
   ISBN 1-56847-423-7
   1. Soviet Union—History—Revolution, 1917–1921—
Juvenile literature. [1. Soviet Union—History—Revolution, 1917–1921.]
I. Title. II. Series: Revolution! (Thomson Learning (Firm))
DK265.G4217   1995
947.084—dc20   95-21918

Printed in Italy

Picture Acknowledgments
The publishers would like to thank the following for permission to use their pictures in this book (t = top, b = bottom, l = left, r = right):
AKG 19; Novosti/Bridgeman Art Library, London *cover*; Camera Press 45(b); Hulton Deutsch 4(t), 5, 6, 16(t), 20(t), 21, 24(t), 25(b), 27, 28, 29(t), 30, 33(b), 40(t), 43(t): David King *title page, contents page,* 4(b), 7, 8, 9(t), 9(b), 10(t), 10(b), 11, 12, 13(t), 13(b), 14(t), 14(b), 15, 18, 20, 22, 23(t), 23(b), 25(t), 26, 29(b), 31, 32, 33(t), 34, 35(t), 36, 37(t), 37(b), 38, 39, 40(b), 41(t), 41(b), 42, 43(b), 44, 45(t); Popperfoto 16(b), 35(b).

CONTENTS

STORMING THE WINTER PALACE

Rumors of revolution spread through the Russian capital city of Petrograd. It was November 1917, and the ruling Provisional Government was on the verge of collapse. Meanwhile, the extreme left-wing Bolshevik Party prepared for open insurrection. The Bolshevik leader, Vladimir Ilyich Lenin, instructed the soldiers supporting him, called Red Guards, to be ready to take over key places in the city. The Bolsheviks were on the point of seizing control of Russia.

Below: *A battalion of women's troops like these were among the few defenders of the Winter Palace on the night of November 6.*

Lenin's supporter, Leon Trotsky, won over the government troops in the great Peter-Paul fortress. The warship *Aurora*, under Bolshevik control, steamed up the Neva River to Petrograd and took up position beside the Winter Palace, which was the headquarters of the Provisional Government.

During the night of November 6, Bolsheviks took control of important bridges and the telegraph station in Petrograd. There was little resistance. The following morning, the main railroad stations were seized, as was the electrical station and the State Bank. All that remained now was the Winter Palace.

In the evening, the government ministers sheltering in the Winter Palace were protected only by a few officer cadets and part of a women's battalion. Small groups of Red soldiers and sailors managed to slip past the defenders and into the palace. In the growing confusion, the Bolsheviks grew

Right: *Lenin sits at his desk looking through the communist party newspaper, called* Pravda, *which means "truth."*

UNDER ARREST

Semion L. Maslov was Minister of Agriculture when the Provisional Government was deposed by the Bolsheviks. Maslov described how the ministers were put under arrest (although they were later released):

"The armed mob of soldiers, sailors and civilians, led by Antonov, broke in. They shouted threats and made jokes. Antonov arrested everybody in the name of the Revolutionary Government…

'We were placed under arrest and told that we would be taken to the Peter-Paul fortress. Each of us was guarded by two men. As we walked through the palace it seemed as if it were filled with the insurrectionists, some of whom were drunk. When we came out on the street we were surrounded by a mob, shouting and threatening.

"At the Troitsky bridge the mob recovered its voice and shouted: 'Throw them into the river!' The calls were becoming louder and louder. Just then a machine gun opened fire from the other side of us. We threw ourselves down, while some of the mob ran, and with them one of the arrested officers." [1]

bolder. Around 11 p.m. the final assault was ordered. Soon the Bolsheviks were marching through the palace corridors in search of the members of the Provisional Government.

In the early hours of the morning, one of the Red Guard commanders, Vladimir Antonov-Ovseyenko, flung open the doors of the chamber where the ministers were sheltering. Antonov loudly proclaimed: "In the name of the Military and Revolutionary Committee of the Petrograd Soviet, I declare the Provisional Government deposed!" [2] With these words, the Bolsheviks seized power.

The whole coup had been achieved with very little bloodshed. The *Aurora* had fired only blank shots and, in the streets of Petrograd, fighting was limited to a few exchanges of rifle fire. Trotsky later wrote that he felt a sense of anti-climax at these events: "The final act of revolution seems, after all this, too brief, too dry, too businesslike." [3]

Below: *Crowds flock around a speaker during one of the many demonstrations that took place outside the Winter Palace, home of the Provisional Government, in 1917.*

RUSSIA UNDER THE CZARS

The Bolshevik Revolution brought an end to centuries of rule by the Russian imperial family, the Romanovs. When Nicholas II became czar of Russia in 1894, he was the ruler of a vast empire that stretched from the borders of Germany eastward to the Pacific Ocean. The empire was made up of many different national and ethnic groups, so that, out of a population of 170 million people, less than half were Russians. The Russian state imposed strict rule over the other national groups. Many resented this, especially in the west where Poles, Ukrainians, Finns, Estonians, Latvians, and Lithuanians demanded independence.

St. Petersburg (renamed Petrograd in 1914) and Moscow were Russia's two main cities. But the vast majority of people lived off the land. Over eighty percent of the population were peasants, badly educated and living in conditions of terrible poverty. Little more than slaves to their rich masters, the peasants were receptive to revolutionary new ideas.

Right: *A map of Russia in the time of Czar Nicholas II. The empire was a mix of different races and nationalities, many of whom opposed the domination by those of Russian origin.*

Below: *The nomadic Kirghiz people lived in the Siberian steppes in tents like this. Their lives of poverty contrasted starkly with the wealthy lifestyles of the aristocracy.*

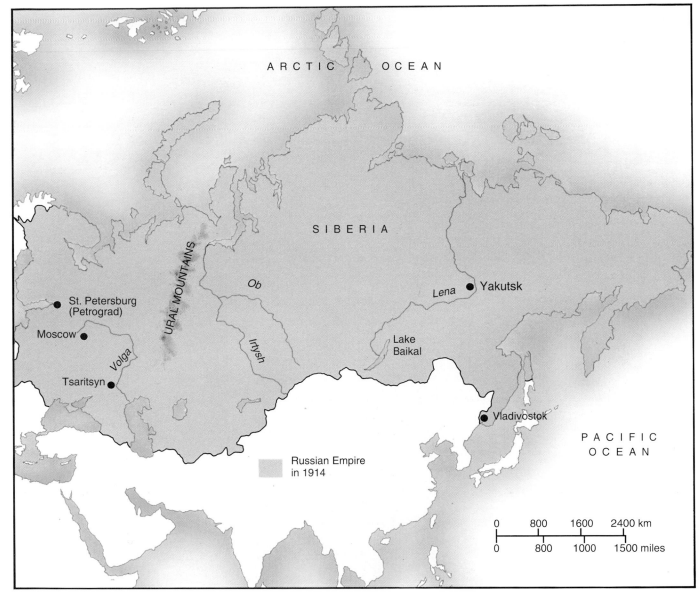

ARCTIC OCEAN

SIBERIA

Ob

Lena • Yakutsk

URAL MOUNTAINS

St. Petersburg
(Petrograd) •

Moscow •

Irtysh

Volga

Tsaritsyn •

Lake
Baikal

Vladivostok •

PACIFIC
OCEAN

Russian Empire
in 1914

| 0 | 800 | 1600 | 2400 km |
| 0 | 800 | 1000 | 1500 miles |

Left: *Having lived in poverty
and oppression for centuries, the
peasants wanted full rights to
their own land and to be freed
from debt repayments to the
great landowners.*

The Czar

In stark contrast to the grinding poverty of most of the population, the Russian nobility lived in splendor. The czar had total power as a ruler. Like his father, Nicholas II believed that he ruled through the will of God. After his coronation, he stated: "Let all know that I, devoting all my strength to the welfare of the people, will uphold the principle of autocracy as firmly and as unflinchingly as my late unforgettable father." [4]

In fact, the czar did little to help his people. He ruled as an autocrat, that is, a monarch who rules without any limit on his authority. The czar's power was maintained through the bureaucracy. This was a system of organization made up of a vast web of officials who ran the empire. Large and cumbersome, the bureaucracy was riddled with corruption. A powerful secret police force, called the *Okhrana*, ensured the obedience of the people. Any protest against the czar was dealt with ruthlessly, and executions and imprisonment were standard ways of tackling unrest. The powerful Russian army was also under the czar's control and could be used to enforce his authority over the people.

Below: *Czar Nicholas and Czarina Alexandra with their children*

Left: *The members of the Duma assemble for its first sitting in May 1906. The Duma had no chance of success because the czar refused to allow it to make decisions.*

Below: *A May Day poster symbolizing the unity of the workers (with hammer) and the peasants (with sickle). The hammer and sickle became a well-known communist image.*

OPPOSITION TO THE CZAR

One important effect of the czar's repressive regime was to make opposition groups illegal. This forced them to operate underground. The repressive activities of the secret police made these groups increasingly radical.

The largest opposition group was the Socialist Revolutionary Party, which had widespread support among the peasants. Much smaller was the Social Democratic Party, which adopted Marxism, the ideas of the German philosopher Karl Marx. Marx believed in a socialist revolution that would be led by the working class against the property-owning capitalists. The socialists believed that, once the revolution had succeeded, the wealth of the country would be shared equally among the people.

In 1903 the Social Democratic Party split into two wings—the moderate Mensheviks and the radical Bolsheviks. Under the determined leadership of Lenin, the Bolsheviks stressed the importance of a small but well-organized and dedicated party.

In the years leading up to the outbreak of World War I in 1914, the efforts made to increase Russia's industrial production began to show results. Financed by large foreign loans, Russian heavy industry began to expand very quickly. By 1914, Russia had become an important industrial nation. As a result, many people moved to the cities to find work. There they were exposed to the revolutionary ideas circulated by underground political groups. Even though the Russian working class was still fairly small, it had become politically active. Strikes and protests against the czarist system were common.

Faced by opposition from most of the Russian people, the czarist empire increasingly relied on its secret police and the armed forces to keep control. If their power was weakened, the entire regime could be overthrown. The outbreak of war against Germany in 1914 placed great strain on this system.

Below: *The wealth of Russian industrialists like these was in dramatic contrast to the desperate poverty experienced by the workers.*

Above: *Life for a coal miner was grim, with low pay and dangerous working conditions. Miners were among the most radical of Russia's workers, and strikes in the coalfields were common.*

Left: *These workers staged a strike in 1905, during the first wave of rebellion. Many more workers were to follow suit in the years before World War I.*

THE WORKERS PREPARE FOR REVOLUTION

The growing mood of radicalism within Russia's working class was revealed in this government report investigating the strikes that occurred through the summer and autumn of 1913: "They happen sometimes for the most trivial causes, and with extraordinary rapidity embrace wide areas with tens of thousands of workers. Under the influence of agitators and the Social Democratic press, there has recently developed among the workers a harmony of action such as indicates their close solidarity and organized nature.

"The places where strikes take place are put under a boycott; those workers who approach are exposed to bitter persecution and are excluded from work. Orders at strikebound factories and plants are also placed under a boycott, and any factory that might accept them risks a strike among its own workers." [5]

WAR AND REVOLUTION

Czar Nicholas II signed the declaration of war against Germany and Austria in August 1914 at the start of World War I. There were high hopes that the vast Russian armies would gain a quick and decisive victory. But from the start, the Russians proved incompetent and defeat followed defeat. Between 1914 and the end of 1916, approximately fifteen million men served in the Russian army and almost half became casualties. Although Russian soldiers were famed for their courage and endurance, such terrible losses lowered the spirits of the Russian forces.

Below: *A long column of Russian prisoners marches into captivity under guard from their German captors.*

War Takes Its Toll

The main cause of the army's problems lay in the poor quality of its leadership and in the failure to get arms and equipment to frontline troops. Russian soldiers often went into battle without rifles and ammunition and were told to pick up weapons found lying on the battlefield. These disasters caused deep humiliation to the Russian people, and anger was directed at the generals and government ministers responsible for the blunders.

Below: *Holding an icon (a religious picture), Czar Nicholas blesses his troops before they go into battle during the early stages of World War I.*

By the end of 1916, the Russian economy was showing signs of serious strain. The railroad system was breaking down, and food shipments into the cities were decreasing. Further hardship was caused by rising prices. The poor were unable to buy basic foods, which were increasingly scarce and expensive. Riots over bread shortages occurred in St. Petersburg (which had been renamed Petrograd in 1914, because St. Petersburg sounded too German), and some army units refused to fight.

When he heard of the riots in Petrograd, Czar Nicholas, away at army headquarters, sent for troops to put down the disturbances. The czar's cavalry arrived in the streets of Petrograd on March 9–10, 1917. They were ordered to disperse the demonstrators but, to everyone's surprise, the troops refused to act and most went over to the demonstrators' side. The situation became critical for the czarist authorities when other military units mutinied. The men of the Volynsky regiment refused orders and shot their own commanding officer. The main Petrograd garrison marched out into the streets clamoring for bread and the end of autocratic rule. The Duma began to call for the czar to abdicate. Outraged, Nicholas demanded the closure of the Duma, but it defied his orders.

TIME LINE

1914
August–September: At the start of World War I, Russian armies are destroyed at the battles of Tannenburg and the Masurian Lakes.

1915
May: The Russians are flung back in defeat after the Austro-German victory at Gorlice-Tarnow.
August: Czar Nicholas II takes over supreme command of the Russian armed forces.

1916
September–October: A wave of strikes sweeps through Petrograd, and demonstrators protest at poor living conditions.

1917
March 8: More demonstrations and strikes break out in Petrograd.
March 12: The Duma forms a committee to replace the czarist government. The Petrograd soviet is formed.
March 15: Czar Nicholas II abdicates.
April: Lenin arrives in Petrograd, via Finland, from exile in Switzerland.
May: The Provisional Government is reorganized, leading to the departure of conservative politicians, replaced by Socialist Revolutionaries and Mensheviks.

Alarmed at the seriousness of the disturbances, Nicholas attempted to return to the capital. Before he could reach Petrograd, however, striking railroad workers took control of the tracks, and the Czar decided to proceed to Pskov, the headquarters of the northern front, instead. There, Nicholas heard about the mutiny of the Volynsky regiment and the collapse of order in Petrograd. Workers' representatives arrived to discuss the possible abdication of Nicholas. Exhausted, the last Russian czar hesitated for only a short while before abdicating on March 15, 1917. He wrote: "To save Russia and keep the army at the front, I decided upon this step.... I left Pskov with heavy feelings; around me treachery, cowardice, and deceit." [6]

Even before Nicholas abdicated, the Duma had begun to call itself the

Above: *Russian workers working on a freight train. The ability of the soviets to control much of Russia's transportation system gave them effective power over the Provisional Government.*

Provisional Government of Russia and, following the departure of Czar Nicholas, it swiftly took over. Most of the members of the Provisional Government were middle-class people who wanted only limited political change. There was just one moderate socialist, Aleksandr Kerensky, but through his talents as a speaker and organizer Kerensky assumed a leading role during the summer of 1917.

The Power of the Soviets

Almost immediately, the Provisional Government faced competition for power from the soviets, which sprang up across the country. The most influential was the Petrograd soviet, which was made up of workers, soldiers, and sailors. It was more radical than the Provisional Government. Throughout the summer of 1917 the soviets and the Provisional Government existed uneasily side by side in what was called the "dual power."

Ultimately, real power lay with the soviets who, through the workers, controlled the transportation system and many of the nation's industrial resources. This fact was recognized by the Provisional Government, and the Minister for War, Aleksandr Guchkov, who said: "The Provisional Government does not possess any real power; and its directives are carried out only to the extent that it is permitted by the Soviet of Workers' and Soldiers' Deputies, which enjoys all the essential elements of real power, since the troops, the railheads, the mail, and the telegraph are all in its hands. One can say flatly that the Provisional Government exists only so long as it is permitted by the soviet.' [7]

Below: *A packed meeting of the Executive Committee of the Petrograd soviet, held inside the Duma building. The main radical political parties tried to influence the Petrograd soviet.*

ALEKSANDR KERENSKY (1881–1970)

After studying law in St. Petersburg, Kerensky became a critical opponent of the czarist system when he was elected to the Duma in 1912 as a moderate socialist. After the abdication of Czar Nicholas, Kerensky entered the Provisional Government, first as Minister of Justice, then as War Minister and from July 1917 Prime Minister.

Although a good organizer and speaker, Kerensky failed to judge the mood of the Russian people in 1917. He ignored their desire for peace, and he failed to introduce a Constituent Assembly to arrange democratic elections. Kerensky greatly underestimated the threat posed by the Bolsheviks and, when they struck in November 1917 and the Provisional Government collapsed, he was deposed. He managed to escape imprisonment, and spent the rest of his life in exile, first in France and then, from 1940 until his death in 1970, in the United States.

Above: *Aleksandr Kerensky*

The Provisional Government made promises that it could not deliver. It was unable to solve the grave economic crisis; food shortages continued and people began to starve. The peasants' demand for their own land intensified, and during 1917 they began to attack landowners and seize property for themselves. One peasant explained: "The land must belong to those who work it with their hands, to those whose sweat flows." [8]

Left: *Photographs of the members of the Provisional Government, shown with the Winter Palace in the background*

At the root of the Provisional Government's problems was its determination to continue fighting the Germans. The Russian people were tired of war and had no wish to continue fighting. Mutinies of army and naval units became more frequent, and German and Austrian troops pushed farther into Russia.

While the Provisional Government became increasingly unpopular, a new force began to emerge. Russia in 1917 was full of extreme socialist parties but they had little influence or power. The Bolsheviks, however, were becoming increasingly popular. Thanks to a new freedom of speech granted by the Provisional Government, Bolsheviks were now allowed to state their views publicly.

Below: *Deserters from the Russian army take over a train to take them back to their homes in Russia.*

THE PROVISIONAL GOVERNMENT

The Provisional Government was a coalition, a group of people from many different political parties. This explains why there was so much argument within the government, and why it was so hard for it to develop an organized policy for dealing with Russia's problems.

The most conservative of the main parties in the Provisional Government were the Octobrists, who had been formed after the 1905 rebellion. They wanted only very limited change. The Cadets (an abbreviation of Constitutional Democrats) argued for a type of democratic government similar to that found in France and Great Britain and were supported by the middle classes. The Labor Party was a moderate socialist party. Although small in numbers, it was well known because it was led by Kerensky.

The Social Revolutionaries had gained a strong following among the peasants, and they demanded the end of private ownership of land. The Marxist Social Democrats were represented in the Provisional Government by the Menshevik wing. The more radical Bolsheviks were totally against the Provisional Government. They preferred to work with the soviets and attack the government in newspapers and leaflets.

VLADIMIR ILYICH LENIN (1870–1924)

Born into a comfortable middle-class family in central Russia, Lenin's political outlook was deeply influenced by the execution of his older brother, Alexander, for his part in the assassination of Czar Alexander II in 1887. In 1897, in St. Petersburg, Lenin was arrested for revolutionary activities and exiled to Siberia for three years. Afterward he spent most of his time abroad, traveling through Europe, meeting and talking with other socialists. Lenin returned to Russia secretly to take part in the 1905 uprising, but in 1906, after the failure of the rebellion, he fled back to Switzerland.

In April 1917, Lenin returned to Russia. He traveled across Europe in a sealed train provided by the German army. The Germans helped socialist agitators like Lenin to return to Russia because most of the agitators didn't want to continue the war against Germany. Lenin immediately devoted himself to the overthrow of the Provisional Government. Lenin was

seen as an eccentric figure, but he was charming, and few people doubted his determination. Although Lenin found fame as a Marxist thinker and writer, his historical importance rests on his practical skills of political and party organization.

John Reed, an American journalist sympathetic to the Bolshevik cause, gave this impression of Lenin: "A short, stocky figure, with a big head set down on his shoulders, bald and bulging. Little eyes, a snubbish nose, wide generous mouth, and heavy chin; clean shaven now but already beginning to bristle with the well-known beard of his past and future.... A strange popular leader—a leader purely by virtue of his intellect; colorless, humorless, uncompromising and detached, without picturesque idiosyncrasies—but with the power of explaining profound ideas in simple terms..." [9]

Right: *Lenin (seated behind the desk) meeting with leading Russian socialists*

THE BOLSHEVIK REVOLUTION

The return of Lenin to Petrograd in April 1917, following a period of exile, signaled the beginning of a new phase in the Revolution. Lenin proposed a simple campaign, aimed at the workers. Under his famous slogans of "Peace! Bread! Land!" and "All power to the soviets!" he urged the people to show their opposition toward the Provisional Government. Lenin was determined that the Bolsheviks must prepare for a revolution as soon as possible, although many of his comrades (fellow Bolsheviks) wanted to wait and let the Provisional Government carry out its more moderate aims.

Lenin set about convincing his comrades that he was right. He met with opposition from Bolsheviks like Grigory Zinoviev and Lev Kamenev, but by reasoned argument he slowly won them over to his side.

By force of personality, Lenin persuaded his followers that a revolution—violent or otherwise—would be successful. But before it could take place, he argued, the Provisional Government must be brought to the point of collapse. In one of his many attacks on the Provisional Government, Lenin summed up the mood of the time: "The people need peace; the people need bread; and the people need land. And they [the Provisional Government] give you war, hunger... and leave the landlords on the land." [10]

Above: *Kamenev (left) and Zinoviev stand beneath a monument to Marx and Engels, the major theorists of communism.*

Right: *Bolshevik agitators spread leaflets through the streets of Petrograd in an attempt to discredit the Provisional Government.*

1917

July 16–18: A premature Bolshevik uprising, known as the July Days, fails to overthrow the Provisional Government.
September 6–10: A right-wing coup, led by General Kornilov, collapses in disorder. The Bolsheviks play a leading role in resisting Kornilov.
November 6–7: The Bolshevik Revolution. The Bolsheviks overthrow the Provisional Government in Petrograd.
December 17: The Bolsheviks get agreement from Germany and Austria for a truce.

1918

January 18: The Constituent Assembly meets, but is immediately closed down by the Bolsheviks.

The July Days

During the spring of 1917 the Bolsheviks began to make political progress, criticizing the Provisional Government and building up influence within the soviets. In July, discontent among the people reached a peak, as the streets of Petrograd again filled with demonstrators demanding cheap food and political change. Although Lenin was not sure that the time was right, the Bolsheviks attempted to topple the government on July 15–16. In what became known as the July Days, the Provisional Government clamped down on the Bolsheviks. Trotsky and other leaders were thrown into jail and Lenin only escaped arrest by wearing a disguise and fleeing to the safety of Finland.

The events of the July Days came as a shock to Lenin and the Bolshevik leadership, but they turned out to be only a temporary setback. While the Bolsheviks recovered, the Provisional Government continued to lurch from crisis to crisis. On August 1, Prime Minister Kerensky appointed General Lavr Kornilov as the new Commander-in-Chief of the Russian army. Kornilov was shocked at the poor discipline of his forces, and with a small group of senior officers he planned to overthrow the Provisional Government and impose military rule over Russia.

Above: *General Kornilov addresses the troops of the Russian army in July 1917.*

Kornilov's Coup

On September 7, Kornilov wrote to Kerensky, demanding that he resign as prime minister. Fearing a right-wing coup, Kerensky turned to the Bolsheviks for help, as they were the only organization capable of fighting against military units. He allowed 25,000 Red Guards to carry

weapons and lifted some of the restrictions on the Bolsheviks. But, before fighting broke out, Kornilov was arrested by government forces and his troops scattered. The failed Kornilov coup was a great help to the Bolsheviks. Not only had they been given permission to operate freely, but their decisive stand against Kornilov had also brought them increased support. At the end of September, the Bolsheviks won majorities in elections to the Moscow and Petrograd soviets.

Above: Soldiers fire on a crowd of demonstrators during the attempted Bolshevik coup of the July Days.

Right: Bolshevik rebels display their firearms on the back of a truck. The Bolsheviks were prepared to take armed action to secure power.

Delighted by this turn of events, Lenin, still in Finland, urged his followers to prepare for an insurrection. Many Bolsheviks recommended caution, but Lenin was insistent that the Bolsheviks' time had come. He said, "History will not forgive us if we do not take power now." [11] Returning to Petrograd, Lenin arranged a secret Bolshevik meeting on November 4 (October 23 in the Julian calendar). Lenin convinced his comrades to rebel and they planned how they would seize power. The meeting was so hurriedly called that the orders for the coup had to be scribbled on the only paper available—a child's lesson book.

At the end of 1917 Petrograd was in a state of turmoil, as rumors of coups and counter-coups spread across the city. Deserters roamed the streets, and soldiers and sailors began to turn on unpopular officers, murdering the most brutal. Workers were taking over their factories, while the managers looked on helplessly. The slogan, "All power to the soviets!" was beginning to have real meaning. Released from prison, Leon Trotsky was elected head of the Petrograd soviet and, working closely with Lenin, he drew up plans for the armed uprising.

Right: *The czar's palace in the Kremlin, Moscow, after an attack by revolutionaries. Despite these isolated outbursts, there was relatively little loss of life and damage to property during the October Revolution.*

Below: *Striking workers at the Putilov factory. The period before the Bolshevik Revolution was one of strikes and demonstrations that helped create an air of instability that the Bolsheviks were able to exploit.*

The October Revolution

The coup was timed to coincide with the All-Russian Congress of Soviets, a conference of all the soviets from around the country. The Bolsheviks controlled 390 of the 650 seats and were determined to get the conference to call for the soviets to assume power in Russia.

On November 6 (October 24, Julian calendar) Red Guards and Bolshevik organizers began to take up positions throughout Petrograd, and during the evening they took over the city. The next day they moved on the Provisional Government, arresting the ministers in the Winter Palace. Meanwhile, the Congress of Soviets voted in favor of the insurrection, and the message was telegraphed across Russia. In other cities the takeover by the soviets was not so easy; in Moscow, for example, five hundred people were killed in street fighting. But the result was clear—the Bolshevik-led soviets had successfully deposed the Provisional Government.

THE FIRST SPARK OF REVOLUTION

Although strikes were illegal in Russia, they were a regular feature of everyday life in Petrograd between October 1916 and November 1917 and become increasingly violent. This police memorandum described the activities taking place on March 8, which was, in effect, the first day of the Russian Revolution:

"On March 8 at 9 a.m. the workers of the plants and factories of the Vyborg district went on strike in protest against the shortage of black bread in bakeries and groceries. The strikes spread to some plants located in the Petrograd, Rozhdestvensky, and Liteny districts, and in the course of the day fifty industrial enterprises ceased work; 87,534 men on strike.

"At about 1 p.m. the workmen of the Vyborg district, walking out in crowds into the street and shouting 'Give us bread,' started to become disorderly in various places at the same time, taking with them on their way their comrades who were at work and stopping streetcars. The demonstrators took away the keys to the electric motors from the streetcars, which forced 15 to quit the lines and retire to Petrograd streetcar yard.

"The strikers, who were resolutely chased by the police and troops summoned for this purpose, were dispersed in one place but quickly gathered in other places, showing themselves to be exceptionally stubborn. In the Vyborg district, order was restored only toward 7 p.m." [12]

REPORTING THE REVOLUTION

The American journalist John Reed provided this eyewitness account of the first few hours of the Bolshevik Revolution:

"Toward four in the morning I met Zorin [a Bolshevik] in the outer hall, a rifle slung over his shoulder. 'We're moving!' said he, calmly, but with satisfaction. 'We pinched the Assistant Minister of Justice and the Minister of Religions. They're down in the cellar now. One regiment is on the march to capture the Telephone Exchange, another the Telegraph Agency, another the State Bank. The Red Guard is out...' On the steps of the Smolny [Bolshevik headquarters], in the chill dark, we first saw the Red Guard—a huddled group of boys in workmen's clothes, carrying guns with bayonets, talking nervously together.

"Far over the roofs westward came the sound of scattered rifle fire, where the yunkers [officer cadets] were trying to open the bridges over the Neva, to prevent the factory workers and soldiers from the Vyborg quarter from joining the Soviet forces in the center of the city.... Behind us great Smolny, bright with lights, hummed like a gigantic hive." [14]

A New Regime

Lenin quickly took advantage of this success. He established his new government, consisting of the Soviet Central Executive Committee and a smaller cabinet of the Council of People's Commissars. Without delay, the Bolshevik program got under way. Banks were nationalized by force; the wealth of the church was seized and it was widely persecuted; titles and ranks were abolished; women were granted equal status with men; and the peasants were given the right to take land from the landowners.

More difficult for the Bolsheviks than issuing orders was the fulfillment of their promise of democratic elections to the Constituent Assembly. Realizing that the Bolshevik position was far from secure because of the threat from right-wing groups, Lenin reluctantly agreed to elections in November. The results were disappointing for the new government. Out of a possible 707 seats, the Bolsheviks won only 175.

Above: *Citizens casting their votes for the first Constituent Assembly in 1918, which was dissolved by Lenin when the votes went against the Bolsheviks*

Afraid that the Bolsheviks would lose power, Lenin gave up the idea of parliamentary democracy. On January 18, the first day that the new Constituent Assembly was due to meet, Bolshevik Red Guards interrupted the session and dissolved the assembly. In justification of their actions, Trotsky launched a ferocious attack against the Assembly: "You are a mere handful, miserable and bankrupt! Your role is finished and you may go where you belong—the garbage dump of history!" [13]

The dissolution of the Constituent Assembly was a step on the road to dictatorship. Yet the Bolsheviks were faced by enormous dangers from outside. The German army continued to press deep into Russia, while the forces of the Russian right wing were regrouping to gather weapons and men to destroy the socialists. These matters were to dominate the thinking of Lenin and his fellow commissars.

Above: *German troops enter Minsk in their bid to seize vast areas of the old Russian empire.*

Right: *Red Army soldiers remove religious objects from a Russian church. Communists were against religion, regarding it as a way of keeping the poor under the control of the capitalist state.*

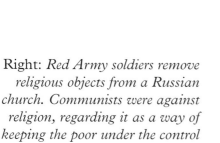

CIVIL WAR

One of the promises made by the Bolsheviks (who early in 1918 began to call themselves communists) was to end the war with Germany. They kept their promise and, after the November coup, a delegation was sent to arrange a peace treaty. The Germans knew they had the upper hand and ruthlessly exploited their position. In March 1918, the two sides met at the small Polish town of Brest-Litovsk, where the Russians had to accept a humiliating peace treaty. Russia lost Poland, Finland, Estonia, Lithuania, Latvia, and Transcaucasia, all of which became German or German protectorates. Russia also lost the agricultural heartland of the Ukraine, and had to give up 80 percent of its sugar factories, 73 percent of its iron, and 75 percent of its coal supply sources.

The Treaty of Brest-Litovsk was very unpopular in Russia, and many communists argued against accepting the Germans' terms. Lenin, however, was determined that Russia must have peace, whatever the price. He told the Petrograd soviet: "To carry on a revolutionary war, an army is necessary, and we do not have one. It is a question of signing terms now, or of signing the death of the Soviet government three weeks later." [15]

TIME LINE

1918
March 3: The new communist government signs the treaty of Brest-Litovsk.
March 5: British troops land at Murmansk in support of White Russian forces.
May: White Russian forces make some gains in southern Russia.
July 16: Nicholas II and his family are shot by Bolsheviks.
August: An attempt is made on Lenin's life by a Socialist Revolutionary named Fanya Kaplan.
November 18: Admiral Kolchak sets up a government in the Urals.

1919
April: The Red Army defeats Kolchak's forces in the east.
October: Denikin's advance on Moscow is halted.

1920
May: Polish forces advance into the Ukraine.
June: Red Army forces retake the Ukraine and advance on Poland.
August 16: Polish troops counterattack south of Warsaw and drive the Red Army out of Poland.
November: The remains of the last White Russian army are thrown out of Russia.

Left: *The German delegation (on the left) forced a humiliating peace on the Russians at Brest-Litovsk.*

Right: *Fanya Kaplan, who attempted to assassinate Lenin in 1918*

Below: *This map shows Russia in 1918–19, following the Bolshevik Revolution.*

The communists were few in number and their hold on power in Russia remained far from safe. Lenin himself was the victim of an assassination plot in August 1918. A disgruntled Socialist Revolutionary supporter named Fanya Kaplan managed to get close to Lenin and fired several shots, two of which penetrated his neck and lungs. Lenin survived, but it was a shock to man whose health was not good to start with.

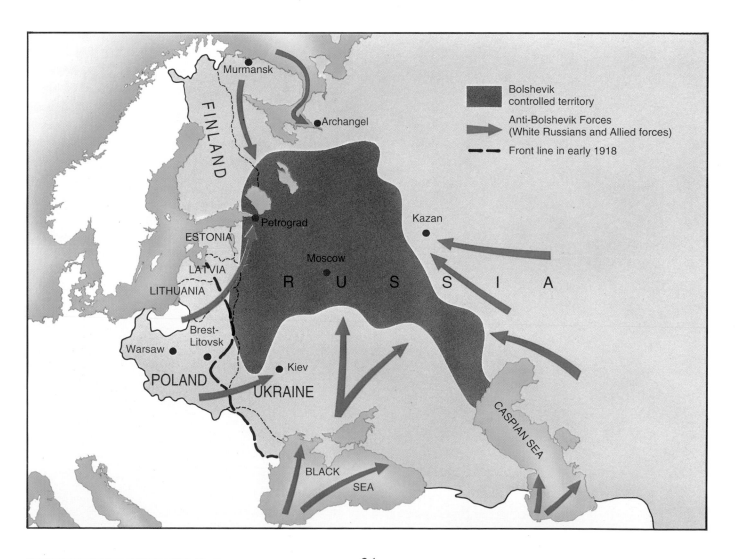

Bolshevik controlled territory

Anti-Bolshevik Forces (White Russians and Allied forces)

Front line in early 1918

The White Threat

Resistance to the new regime was fierce, especially from the many non-Russian nationals who were eager to use the turmoil caused by the revolution to form their own independent states. More serious, however, was the threat from Russians who hated communist rule. Known as "Whites" (as opposed to the "Red" communists), their forces gathered on the borders of the country, where they received support from Western nations, such as Great Britain, France, and the United States. These countries were against communism and wanted to restore the Provisional Government, which had continued the war against Germany.

The outrage felt by the West toward the communists was increased by the death of Czar Nicholas and his family on July 16, 1918. They were shot by a Red Army firing squad, for reasons which have never been explained. It is possible that the communists feared that the czar might be freed by White forces and would become the focus of anti-communist feeling.

Right: *A communist poster celebrates the triumph of the Red Army over White forces. During the civil war, the Red Army became a powerful fighting force several million strong.*

A CRUEL WAR

The civil war was fought with great brutality on both sides. This account from an onlooker describes the behavior of White forces after they had recaptured an area from Red troops: "The mounted platoon entered the village, met the Bolshevik committee, and put the members to death.... After the execution the houses of the culprits were burned and the male population under forty-five whipped soundly.... Then the population was ordered to deliver without pay the best cattle, pigs, fowl, forage, and bread for the whole detachment, as well as for the best horses." [16]

Above: *The White Russian commander, Admiral Kolchak, who attacked the Bolsheviks from the east, over the Ural Mountains*

Initially, the White Russians made good progress against the communists. In southern Russia and the Ukraine, troops under General Anton Denikin advanced steadily toward Moscow; in the east, Admiral Aleksandr Kolchak crossed the Ural mountains. In the north, the Western allies set up a new opposition Russian government in Archangel. Between the summer of 1918 and early 1919, it looked as though the communist regime would fall to the White forces.

Right: *British troops on the Murmansk-Archangel front. To many Russians, the attacks on the communists by Western powers were seen as a foreign invasion, and the Whites lost support as a result.*

The communists were saved by four factors. First, the White Russians had no organized aims, and they did not work together in fighting the Reds. Second, the communists had the advantage of operating from the central bases of Petrograd and Moscow. In contrast, the Whites were forced to fight around the edges, with large distances separating their forces. Third, by accepting Western aid, the Whites were seen by the people as working for foreign powers, while the communists claimed to be patriots saving Russia. And fourth, the communists had, in Leon Trotsky, a talented military leader who was able to turn his rabble of an army into an effective fighting force of some five million.

Below: *Trotsky inspects troops of the Red Army. As Commissar for War, Trotsky was largely responsible for the communist victory in the civil war. He was a brilliant organizer who imparted energy and discipline into his forces.*

Aided by the brilliant soldier and war hero Mikhail Tukhachevsky, Trotsky was ruthless in building up the Red Army. Conscription (compulsory military service) was reintroduced, and commanders who retreated from battle were shot. Trotsky traveled up and down the country in an armored train, supervising his forces and urging the troops on to greater efforts. Horses were used in great numbers in this brutal war, and whole cavalry armies rode across the countryside, destroying all in their path.

Communist Victory

By the end of 1919, the tide of war had turned against the Whites. General Anton Denikin was driven back and he and the remnants of his army were forced to evacuate from the Black Sea port of Odessa. In the east, Kolchak's forces were defeated and he was captured and shot by Red soldiers. In the autumn of 1920 the remnants of the White Russian army under General Wrangel were forced out of their last stronghold in the Crimea. Standing on the dock with his troops, waiting to embark, Wrangel put a brave face on the disaster: "We are going into exile. We are not going as beggars with outstretched hands, but with our heads held high, conscious of having done our duty till the end." [17] The civil war was over.

In 1919, at the height of the civil war, Poland had taken advantage of the communists' weakened position and had advanced into the Ukraine. Relations between Poland and Russia had been poor, especially since Russian communists were encouraging the workers of Europe to rise up against their governments. In response to the Polish attack, a Red cavalry army pushed deep into Poland, and for a while it looked as if the Polish capital, Warsaw, would fall to the Russians. The Poles rallied, however, and drove the Red Army back in total disorder. The communists were forced to ask for a peace treaty to prevent a military disaster. The Treaty of Riga, signed in March 1921, was a reminder to the communists of the danger of pushing the revolution forward too far, too soon.

Below: *In Moscow's Sverdlov Square on May 5, 1920, Lenin addresses Red Army troops on their way to fight the Poles. Trotsky can be seen standing to the right of the wooden stage.*

THE TRIUMPH OF COMMUNISM

Above: *Labor conscripts assemble for work as part of Lenin's War Communism policy. Not surprisingly, such measures caused widespread discontent.*

In 1921, after seven years of war and revolution, Russia lay in ruins. Industrial production was a small fraction of what it had been in 1914. In the countryside, food was scarce. The need to increase food production, especially to feed the workers in the cities, was a desperate problem for the Soviet government. The peasants were reluctant to part with their produce, and consequently communist patrols were sent into the rural areas to collect food by force. This caused deep bitterness among the peasantry. In the cities, the communists introduced conscription to provide workers for the mines, roads, and rail-building projects. Lenin justified his policies under the heading of "War Communism."

War Communism

With the end of the civil war and the end of external threat from White forces, resentment of the Communist Party increased dangerously. In 1921 there was a revolt by thousands of peasants in the Tambov region south of Moscow, and Red sailors at the naval base of Kronstadt mutinied at the harsh conditions and lack of freedom in Soviet Russia. Both uprisings were crushed severely by General Mikhail Tukhachevsky, and those captured were either shot or sent to labor camps.

Left: *Three of the Red Army's leading commanders (from left): Generals Voroshilov, Budenny, and Tukhachevsky. Of these, Tukhachevsky was the most talented. He was executed on trumped-up charges of treason in 1937 by Lenin's successor, Stalin.*

1921
March: The Kronstadt rebellion is crushed. Lenin introduces the New Economic Policy.

1922
December: Russia becomes the Union of Soviet Socialist Republics (USSR).

1924
January 21: Vladimir Ilyich Lenin dies.

1925
January 16: Trotsky is dismissed as War Minister.

1927
November: Trotsky is expelled from the Communist Party.

1928
The first Five-Year-Plan goes into effect, designed to develop Soviet heavy industries.

1930
Stalin introduces collectivization of Soviet agriculture.

War Communism caused widespread misery, and demands for greater political freedom became increasingly common. This proclamation from striking workers is typical: "A complete change is necessary in the policies of the Government. First of all, the workers and peasants need freedom. They don't want to live by decrees of the Bolsheviks.... Determinedly and in an organized manner [we] demand: liberation of all arrested Socialists; abolition of martial law; freedom of speech, press, and assembly..." [18]

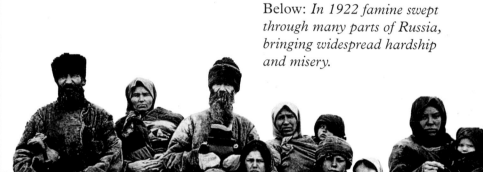

Below: *In 1922 famine swept through many parts of Russia, bringing widespread hardship and misery.*

The New Economic Policy

Although the demands of the workers were not met, they influenced Lenin, who sensed the dangers of continuing with War Communism. In March 1921 he introduced the New Economic Policy (NEP), designed to pacify the rising anger of the people. Grain would no longer be taken by force. Instead, the peasants would pay a tax but would be free to buy and sell their produce as they pleased. Although the NEP helped in the long term, a mass famine swept the country in 1922 and millions of people starved to death. The famine would have been far worse if grain had not been sent to Russia by charities from the United States.

EXPORTING THE REVOLUTION

By the end of 1921, when the Revolution was reasonably secure within Russia, communist leaders had to decide what the next step should be. Some, notably Trotsky, believed in a "permanent revolution," based on the idea that Russian communism could not hope to prosper unless there were similar uprisings throughout the capitalist world.

But this concept of world revolution was opposed by other leaders, who wished to take a more cautious path. The failure of the Red Army in the war against Poland convinced Lenin that Russia was not strong enough to help communism to spread to other countries. This view was accepted and was taken up by Stalin, Lenin's successor, who trumpeted the slogan, "Socialism in one country." He believed that members of the Comintern (Communist International, comprised of communist parties around the world) should merely support communism in Soviet Russia.

Below: *Lenin speaks at the opening of the Second Congress of the Comintern.*

Despite improvements, the NEP also brought increased repression in political and social life. Any criticism of the Communist Party was dealt with harshly, and the *Cheka* (secret police) became as powerful as the czarist secret police in the days before the Revolution. People who spoke out against communism were rounded up by the police and disappeared into labor camps. Increasingly, the Communist Party took over the running of the country, changing from a political party into a bureaucracy for the running of the state. Individuals who wanted to succeed in Soviet Russia had to be members of the Communist Party.

Above: *People line up to buy bread in Moscow, 1921, as the New Economic Policy takes effect.*

The Struggle for Leadership

Lenin's health declined during 1922 and 1923, and a struggle for his successor began to develop. Trotsky was the most brilliant of the communist leaders and was favored by Lenin, but he was not popular in the Party. Grigory Zinoviev was also considered to be a possible successor and, supported by Kamenev, he was determined to beat Trotsky. The most unlikely candidate was Joseph Stalin. He had played only a minor role during the Revolution, but unlike Trotsky and Zinoviev he was very skillful in acquiring power, and he was ruthless in using it.

Stalin built support within the Party during the civil war, and his appointment as General Secretary of the Communist Party in 1922, gave him new opportunities to further his career. As the Communist Party became more important in the organization of the country, Stalin's influence grew. Lenin began to mistrust Stalin, but Lenin's death in January 1924 prevented him from stopping Stalin's ruthless campaign for control of the party.

Below: *An ailing Lenin (left) sits next to his eventual successor, Joseph Stalin. Lenin unsuccessfully attempted to reduce Stalin's influence.*

Right: *Lenin lies in state after his death in January 1924. Lenin's death gave Stalin the opportunity to outwit his opponents in the battle for power in the Communist Party.*

Left: *Members of the feared* Cheka, *the communist secret police, prepare for a May Day parade in 1920.*

LEON TROTSKY (1879–1940)

Trotsky was a revolutionary from an early age. He joined the Russian Social Democrats, but sided with the Mensheviks at the 1903 congress. During the 1905 uprising Trotsky organized the first soviet in St. Petersburg, for which he was arrested and exiled to Siberia. He escaped and traveled to France and then the United States.

On hearing the news of the March rising in 1917, Trotsky returned to Russia and, after a brief period of imprisonment by the Provisional Government, he joined the Bolsheviks. Along with Lenin he was the chief organizer of the November coup, which brought the Bolsheviks to power. He was a leading negotiator at the Treaty of Brest-Litovsk, and in his position as Commissar for War he virtually created the Red Army.

Following his expulsion from the Communist Party, Trotsky was forced to leave Russia in 1929. He continued to attack Stalin in his writings and, eventually, Stalin had Trotsky murdered in his home in Mexico, in 1940.

Right: *Trotsky (seated, second from left) attends the Congress of Soviets in 1918.*

With Lenin out of the way, Stalin set about eliminating his rivals. Allying himself with Zinoviev and Kamenev, and supported by the Party structure, Stalin attacked Trotsky. As Trotsky had only joined the Bolsheviks on the eve of the 1917 Revolution, he did not have much solid support within the Party. Stalin managed to persuade the other leading communists to have Trotsky expelled from the Party in 1927. With Trotsky out of the way, Stalin turned on Zinoviev and Kamenev. They, too, were expelled from the Party and, along with many old Bolshevik leaders, were executed in 1936 on trumped-up charges of treason.

Right: *A poster from a communist literacy campaign compares illiteracy to blindness. The communists made great efforts to improve standards of education in the Soviet Union, and such campaigns were common.*

Stalin ruthlessly crushed anyone who opposed him. The peasants were controlled by the process of collectivization, in which they lost their land to the state and were forced to become agricultural laborers. Industrial workers toiled in the most severe conditions to develop Russia's economy. Millions died from overwork and starvation, but by the 1930s the Soviet Union was a major world power, rivaled in economic strength only by the United States. Stalin, the former Bolshevik revolutionary, now ruled Russia with as much power as had the former autocrat, Czar Nicholas II.

Above: *Trotsky is driven by armed bodyguards in his first-phase of exile in the Caucasus Mountains. His fear of assassination was to prove well-founded.*

JOSEPH STALIN (1879–1953)

Stalin was born in the southern Russian province of Georgia, where he became involved in revolutionary politics. After exile to Siberia in 1904 for revolutionary activities, he joined the Bolshevik wing of the Social Democratic Party. He became editor of the Bolshevik newspaper *Pravda*. Stalin played a relatively minor role in the 1917 Revolution, being described by one Bolshevik as the "gray blur."

After the Revolution, Stalin was appointed Commissar for Nationalities and joined the Central Committee and the *Politbyuro*. In 1922 he became Party Secretary of the Communist Party. Following the death of Lenin in 1924, Stalin outwitted his rivals and effectively became the leader of soviet Russia. Unlike most of his fellow Bolsheviks, Stalin had little interest in international affairs and Marxist theory. His strengths lay in practical politics, and the development of "Socialism in one country," namely the Soviet Union.

COMMUNISM AND THE WORLD

For the people of Russia, the impact of the Revolution was immediate and dramatic. The misery and hardship that followed the Revolution remains one of the more terrible episodes in Russia's long and turbulent history. However, the industrialization of the country by the communists created a superpower. Individual freedoms were brutally reduced, but standards of living rose and people of humble birth had chances to advance to positions of authority.

Many Bolshevik leaders had expected the Revolution to spread to the capitalist West, but communism had little success in Western countries. In part, this was due to Stalin's restraining influence, but mainly it was a result of the economic and political strength of the Western nations, especially those with democratic systems that allowed people to participate in the political process. Only as a result of Soviet military strength after World War II did Eastern Europe come under communist control.

Below: *A poster celebrating Chinese communism in the 1960s. The pilot at the rear of the group is waving the "Little Red Book," which consisted of a collection of revolutionary ideas developed by Mao Tse-tung, the communist leader of China.*

The Spread of Communism

To the surprise of many communists, the influence of Soviet communism was greatest in the underdeveloped nations of the Third World—in Asia, Africa, and South America. These countries had been colonized by Western nations and eagerly adopted the revolutionary ideas offered by communism.

Above: *The two communist leaders, Mao Tse-tung and Nikita Khrushchev (who succeeded Stalin) exchange greetings.*

China was the first and most important Asian state to adopt communism as its political system. Under the leadership of Mao Tse-tung, the Chinese developed their own form of communism, based on the importance of the peasants rather than the industrial workers. The pattern of the Chinese Revolution provided the model for many other communist uprisings, most notably in Vietnam.

However, the influence of Russian communism remained strong throughout the world, especially as the Soviet Union supported other communist governments, from Cuba in the Caribbean to Yemen in the Arabian Peninsula.

The collapse of communism in Eastern Europe and the Soviet Union in the 1990s has changed the way we look at the Russian Revolution. The Revolution cannot be seen as the great success proclaimed for it by communists and their supporters, and yet there can be no denying the importance of this great event in the history of the twentieth century.

Left: *Germans celebrate the destruction of the Berlin Wall in 1989. The wall had separated communist East Berlin from West Berlin since 1961.*

GLOSSARY

Abdicate To give up a high position or office, such as a throne.

Agitator A person who stirs up public feeling on controversial issues.

Allies Countries or organizations that cooperate with each other.

Autocrat A person, usually a monarch or emperor, who has complete and sole power in a country.

Bolshevik A member of the Russian extreme left-wing party led by Lenin. *Bolshevik* means *majority*, although originally the Bolsheviks were a minority in the Social Democratic Party.

Boycott To refuse to have anything to do with another person or organization.

Capitalism An economic and political system in which land, factories, etc. are privately owned and used to make money.

Capitalist A person who owns an industrial or financial concern, such as a factory, bank, or mine, and who tries to make money from it.

Cavalry Soldiers on horseback.

Civilians People who are not in the armed services or police force.

Collectivization A process developed by Stalin in which the peasants were made to work in state farms under the control of the government.

Commissars Russian government officials.

Conscription A system in which people are forced by the state to join the armed forces.

Conservative Believing in keeping things as they are.

Coup A swift and violent change of government, where one group or party replaces another.

Delegation A group of people who put forward the views of a larger group of people.

Democracy Government in which the people have the ruling power through their representatives or through direct ballot.

Deposed Removed from power by force.

Dictatorship A system where power is concentrated in the hands of one person.

Duma The Russian parliament, first elected in 1906, which became the Provisional Government in 1917.

Exile Expulsion from one's own country

Imperial Of an empire (in this case, czarist empire).

Insurrection An uprising by the people against the rulers of a country.

Manifesto A public statement by a monarch or public body, announcing its intentions.

Martial law Military rule.

Moderate In politics, a person whose opinions are not strong or extreme.

Mutinies Revolts of soldiers or sailors against their commanding officers.

Nationalize To place an industrial or financial concern, such as a factory, bank, or railroad system, under the direct control of the state.

Peasant A member of a class of farm workers and farmers with small farms. In Russia the peasants were usually very poor.

Politbyuro The twelve-man political bureau for policy decision-making that was created in 1919 from the Soviet Central Executive Committee.

Radical In politics, a person who holds an extreme view.

Regime A system of government (as in a communist regime).

Repressive Tightly controlled.

Right-wing Having conservative political views.

Socialism The belief that every member of the community should share in the ownership and control of manufacture, finance, and trade.

Soviet The Russian word for an elected council.

Underground Done in secret. An underground organization that works in secret and usually holds radical views.

FURTHER INFORMATION

BOOKS

Caulkins, Janet. *Joseph Stalin*. New York: Franklin Watts, 1990.

Haney, John. *Vladimir Lenin*. World Leaders—Past and Present. New York: Chelsea House, 1988.

Kort, Michael. *The Rise and Fall of the Soviet Union*. New York: Franklin Watts, 1992.

Leone, Bruno, ed. *Communism: Opposing Viewpoints*. San Diego: Greenhaven Press, 1986.

Resnick, Abraham. *Russia: A History to 1917*. Revised edition. Enchantment of the World. Chicago: Childrens Press, 1992.

Ross, Stewart. *The Russian Revolution, 1914–1924*. New York: Franklin Watts, 1989.

Solzhenitsyn, Aleksandr I. *One Day in the Life of Ivan Denisovich*. New York: Bantam Books, 1984. Originally published in the United States in 1963.

For older readers

Fitzpatrick, Sheila. *The Russian Revolution 1917–1932*. New York: Oxford University Press, 1984.

Malamud, Bernard. *The Fixer*. New York: Penguin Books, 1989. Originally published in the United States in 1966.

Hughes, Gwyneth and Welfare, Simon. *Red Empire: The Forbidden History of the U.S.S.R.* New York: St. Martin's Press, 1990.

Reed, John. *Ten Days that Shook the World*. New York: Bantam Books, 1992. A classic account of the revolution by an American journalist who was in Russia at the time and was sympathetic to the Soviets. Originally published in the United States in 1919.

FILMS

Doctor Zhivago directed by David Lean (1965).
   Love story of an idealistic doctor caught up in the turmoil of the Revolution.

The Fixer directed by John Frankenheimer (1968).
   The story of a Jewish man unjustly imprisoned in Czarist Russia.

October directed by Sergei Eisenstein (1928).
   An account of the Bolshevik Revolution.

Potemkin directed by Sergei Eisenstein (1925).
   The story of the mutiny of Russian sailors in the 1905 Revolution.

Reds directed by and starring Warren Beatty (1981).
   The story of American journalist John Reed and his experiences in Russia in 1917.

SOURCES OF QUOTES

1 Quoted in *The Russian Chronicles* (London: Garamond/Random Century Group, 1990).

2 Quoted by Gwyneth Hughes and Simon Welfare in *Red Empire* (St. Martin's Press, 1990).

3 Quoted by Hughes and Welfare in *Red Empire*.

4 Quoted by Stewart Ross in *The Russian Revolution* (Franklin Watts, 1989).

5 Quoted in *The Russian Chronicles*.

6 Quoted by Hughes and Welfare in *Red Empire*.

7 Quoted by Sheila Fitzpatrick in *The Russian Revolution 1917-1932* (Oxford University Press, 1984).

8 Quoted by Hughes and Welfare in *Red Empire*.

9 John Reed in *Ten Days that Shook the World*. (Bantam, 1984).

10 Quoted by Brian Catchpole in *A Map History of Russia* (London: Heinemann, 1988).

11 Quoted by Hughes and Welfare in *Red Empire*.

12 John Reed in *Ten Days that Shook the World*.

13 Quoted by Brian Catchpole in *A Map History of Russia*.

14 John Reed in *Ten Days that Shook the World*.

15 Quoted by Hughes and Welfare in *Red Empire*.

16 Quoted by Stewart Ross in *The Russian Revolution*.

17 Quoted by Hughes and Welfare in *Red Empire*.

18 Quoted by Stewart Ross in *The Russian Revolution*.

INDEX